DECODING GEN-Z SLANG

YOUR GUIDE TO LEARNING, UNDERSTANDING,
AND SPEAKING THE GEN-Z VERNACULAR

DEVON KNOTT

1

AND I OOP?!

What happened that would warrant me writing a book about Gen-Z slang now of all times? Well, how about a once-in-a-century pandemic? I know, I know, I went there right at the start of the book and at this point for many of us the word Covid has become somewhat of a trigger warning, but, hey, I figured if I'm to write this entire thing and then publish it for the world to read, I should provide a reason. A legitimate one, because pointlessly doing things is not the ethos by which I've lived most of my life.

A little about me: I'm Devon, I'm thirty-six as of writing this, and it's the 24th of April, 2021 AD. Or 2 PC. As in Post-Covid.

I can already picture a mental crowd going, "Hey Devon! How are you doing, Devon? Why are you writing this book, Devon? What makes you an authority on the subject matter, Devon?"

Okay crippling-anxiety-inducing mental voices, I shall answer you if you leave me alone to my devices after this moment onward: I'm doing okay, thank you for asking. Why am I writing this book? Hey, didn't I just address this question two paragraphs up? I did. But you want me to expound, elucidate. Fine.

So, a buddy of mine popped over from out of town the other day, Corey. And Corey's infamous for hanging around with a younger crowd. Before you cast aspersions on the noble character of my very nice friend Corey, let me just clarify that I meant young-adults. There. Does that make it better? Fine. Thanks.

So, Corey and I were chatting, as long-time friends do, and he started throwing around these phrases that made my face imitate the timeless stare of Dwayne Johnson, that judgmental thing he does with his eyebrows, you know? The intense stare. Corey looked at me as if I was having some form of stroke, mimicking my facial expressions. In hindsight it was very comical.

Corey had just used some insane words that I hadn't heard before in my entire life. Words like "Yeet." I will reiterate this, folks. I'm thirty-six. It did not occur to me that my friend Corey was not having a stroke. I asked him if there was something wrong with him.

"Yee-yee, whatchu talking about?" And then he lifted both arms up in the air at an angle and dabbed.

Consider me for a second there, back in the drawing room with Corey with his forehead wedged in his elbow, Corey a grown man. Corey, my old friend who'd somehow transcended the need for actual words in a conversation.

I, simpleminded fool that I was back then, asked him what he meant by "Yeet."

"If you don't know, you don't know, and if you have to ask, you're uncool. So, please, Devon. Don't embarrass me right now, my guy."

Worried about my dear friend's mental well-being, I prodded the matter further.

Yo, listen, my dude, it's like this. It's like, you have to understand, these kids, these Gen-Z's, they've formed their own language, much like we'd formed ours in order to communicate covertly in front of our parents. Remember the *Whazzzap* craze? Yeah, multiply it by ten-thousand and then throw away your calculator and buy a super-computer and be prepared to deal with the mathematics of infinity, because that's how big this is.

Yep. My friend had gone insane. I'll miss him.

I asked him to be a bit more coherent with me. I wasn't in the mood for riddles.

"Gen-Z slang is a dictionary unto its own," he told me. "These kids, well, they can't be called kids anymore because Gen-Z is technically everyone born after 1995, that is to say, their childhoods and their adolescence and teenage years, all of them were spent in pretty much the 21st century. So, their language, it's entirely new. In order to communicate with them, you have to learn how they speak."

Okay. This was much more helpful.

At this point in the narrative, I was FOMOing a bit, but not desperately so. That's the *fear of missing out, by the way.*

Folks, at one point in every person's life, they must don the Sherlock cap, put his proverbial pipe in their mouths (No! Not like that!) and become a sleuth. This was my moment to do so.

So, I set out on this journey to make some semblance of sense of this new language, this trend of buzz-words and hashtags and gamer-tags and memes and, well, internet culture.

I shall now present my findings.

I shall do my best to figure out if these words are, in fact, legible, tangible, actual words with meanings behind them or are just nonsensical catchphrases that have devolved language into a pathetic carica-ture of itself.

And this I write as an outsider, because, as I've estab-lished, I'm a millennial. I shall try to understand if this is the same as what happened with my genera-tion and previous generations.

And, yes, since there's something genuinely funny about phrases like "Finsta" and "Stonks," I shall poke fun where necessary. But in good humor. Not as a bitter old man feeling left out or anything. As an amused spectator, you can say.

And I Oop?!

Here's one that I, if I'm understanding it correctly based on the Urban Dictionary explanation, found amusing and relatable enough to make it the title of this chapter.

And I oop. And. I. Oop.

It's an expression you use when you're witness to something that catches you off-guard or catches your attention. Further scrolling down Google provided me with the historical context of this phrase. It was first said by the drag queen Jasmine Masters (from RuPaul's Drag Race) on a video uploaded on YouTube in 2015 and then became viral. Viral enough that the video got viewed around 2 million times. There's a pattern there, folks. You'll see. I've been ooping since I read the definition, and I oop, I hope I've been oopingly loopingly using it the right way. Oops. I'm not.

I think it's quite fitting to use it as the title because, well, this lingo caught me off-guard. But God as my witness, I shall not say "and I oop" any longer to this gibberish. I shall investigate. I shall discover. I shall document my findings and somehow, through sheer willpower, will learn to speak Gen-Z slang better than Gen-Z.

And Corey? Yeah, bro, next time you're in town, you're gonna get a dose of your own medicine, son. Just you watch. I shall take my etymological research, my amazing discovery of this new language that has yet to be documented by a true philologist, and I shall emasculate you with my knowledge.

2

REVENGE OF THE NERDS

Nerd culture has always been around. The term nerd culture itself, however, is a relatively new one. The word "nerd" first originated, historians largely agree, in a Dr. Seuss text called If I Ran the Zoo. The context is an amusing one:

> And then, just to show them, I'll sail to
>   Ka-troo
> And bring back an It-kutch, a Preep and a
>   Proo,
> A Nerkle, a Nerd, and a Seersucker, too!

What was once a slur for an unpopular person with their nose deep in the books, characterized by a stereotypical persona with a window pane width of glass held to their face by a frame equally as bulky, acne ridden skin, drool hanging from their lips, wearing unappealing clothing, and a single-minded obsession with a certain topic is now a universally accepted and reclaimed term for someone who's an absolute master of their craft. Tech giants like Jobs (even though, yes, I agree, Wozniak did all the coding) and Gates and Zuckerberg and Dell started out as nerds. Computer nerds, to be precise. Neil Gaiman can be labeled a nerd of storytelling using that very logic. You can look at Stephen King's career in writing and dub him a horror nerd.

And somewhere along the journey, the nerds won.

Also, that movie, Revenge of the Nerds, is, I believe one of the most underrated movies of all time.

It defies traditional definition these days, the word nerd. Whom you have might have thought of as a very hunky man, say, Henry Cavill, is a certified nerd and a beloved icon of the geeks and the pop-culture fanatics. Case in point, in 2020 his posts of assembling a PC as part of his quarantine pastime became instantaneously viral. Here was Cavill, the person portraying Superman AND Geralt of Rivia, assembling a PC, admitting that one of his favorite activities was turning his rig on and spending count-less hours playing Warhammer.

Regardless of whether he's doing that as a hobby, or as a marketing stunt, the fact remains that this has made him immensely popular among the tech-savvy, the pop-culture enthusiasts, the nerds, and, yes, Gen-Z.

You can easily find Twitter threads "thirsting" over him, which is another word I learned in my research, calling him "daddy" and "pro-gamer."

Another accessible case study is Keanu Reeves.

Keanu Reeves rose to fame in front of us millennials. However, it's pertinent to note that the beloved Keanu was born in 1964, which is the cutoff for Baby Boomers and Gen-X. Is he a Boomer or is he a Gen-Xer? I shall now strive to solve this mystery before I go into the details of what made him famous in the Gen-Z demo.

All right. After doing thorough research, I have deduced that Mr. Reeves was born on the 2nd of September. A year has 12 months in it. September is the 9th month. With me so far? Okay. So, the cutoff for Boomer/Gen-X is June, if my math is correct.

This makes Mr. Reeves a member of the Gen-X community by a hairline.

At the E3 Xbox Conference of 2019, Keanu appeared onstage, dripping mad charisma and all, sporting a nice coat, a rough beard, and his classical long hair. He was going to be part of Cyberpunk 2077, the much-awaited videogame developed by Cd Projekt Red, the same guys behind The Witcher games.

Someone from the crowd yelled, "You're breathtaking!" to which Keanu, in perfect Keanu fashion, pointed at the member of the audience and proclaimed: "No, you're breathtaking."

That.

That was the singular moment in history that made Keanu into a living legend. Forget the Matrix movies, forget that Keanu had done an excellent job alongside Al Pacino in The Devil's Advocate, forget that this was John Wick AND John Constantine. No. To the younger generations, Keanu will always be remembered as the wholesome guy who had appeared onstage and declared his love for the audience.

But how? How?

All right.

Are you ready?

Memes. *They're pronounced meems. Not me-mes.*

If you want to learn Gen-Z slang, you must understand memes. You also have to realize that memes have a spectrum, ranging from dank to normie. The dankest of memes are harvested from Reddit and 4chan. *Dank refers to something extremely cool. Normie, here, implies something so mainstream, so basic, that it's what normal people like.*

There is a trickle-down effect of memes that one must be mindful of when studying this mode of communication.

I am assuming you already know the basics of memes.

The definition from Oxford Languages (I know, I know, starting out about a particular topic with the definition of said topic is the Jim Belushi of writing, but let's let that slide for a bit) states that memes are an image, video, piece of text, etc. typically humorous in nature, that is copied and spread rapidly by internet users, often with slight variations. The origins of the word memes are Greek in nature, derived from the word miméma, which means "that which is irritated."

Now let's expound upon the origin of memes and how they're passed around and what makes a meme viral.

Andy Warhol, famous American director, producer, and artist, stated that, "In the future, everyone will be world-famous for 15 minutes."

If this were a bet, Mr. Warhol, and were it that you were alive, you'd have been a millionaire or bitcoin billionaire, depending on how much money or cryptocurrency you'd have invested in that statement.

Modern day memes originate on Reddit, in subreddits like r/memes and r/dankmemes, and depending upon the subject matter of those memes, other specific subreddits, such as r/lotrmemes, which is a subreddit dedicated to memes related to The Lord of The Rings.

On Reddit, there is a rating system called karma and awards that you can give to other redditors if you decide that their posts are awesome. You can also take away their points if you find something very disturbing.

Why is Reddit integral here? Not only because it has 430 million active monthly users and more than 100,000 active communities, but because it's the hip platform to be on. This in part is due to Reddit's marketing strategy that pitches it as "The front page of the internet." Very much like Twitter, whose tagline is "It's what's happening," Reddit is all about the now.

When Keanu rose to fame because of his "You're breathtaking" comment, it wasn't just because there were practically millions of people tuned in to watch the E3 conference; it was because everyone tuned in to the streams was constantly sharing everything on Twitch, Twitter, Reddit, YouTube, Facebook, Discord, Tumblr, Snapchat, Instagram, and other prominent social media networks.

Already a heartthrob of the masses, Keanu's wholesome persona was memefied and thus made immortal on the internet. The memes originated on Reddit, became upvoted enough to catch the attention of average Reddit users, were passed down to Twitter, Facebook, Instagram, and were then shared in the form of messages with everyone.

It was an inside joke that the entire gaming community was in on.

There must be a resolution to this entire monologue. It is this: The nerds won. The nerds got their revenge. They created the platforms that now millions of people use to communicate with each other in different languages, Gen-Z slang being one of them.

If you're like me, someone who's been out of the loop for some time, and want to catch up on Gen-Z slang, their trends and what's current, I suggest memes. Yes, it'll boggle you for a moment, but sooner than later the analytical part of your brain will kick in and you will start understanding what they're talking about, and as is the case with every language, once you've become fluent enough in understanding it, you can start using it and catch them off-guard. It's all very meta, you must understand. They think we don't understand, but we do. And an understanding of that understanding is the definition of yet another term that they're throwing around casually: Meta.

I would like to build upon the momentum of this chapter and do a transition to gaming slang and how it affects Gen-Z language.

3

F'S IN THE CHAT

On the 4th of November, 2014, a videogame developed by Sledgehammer Games, Raven Software, and High Moon Studios, published by Activision and Square Enix, starring Kevin Spacey (who has since been cancelled into oblivion), had a rather odd cutscene in the first act, a cutscene that led to the viral phrase "F's in the chat."

The game that I speak of is none other than Call of Duty: Advanced Warfare. At that time, the videogame was bashed heavily by critics, garnering a rating of merely 6/10 on Steam. Sure, IGN gave it a 9.1/10, but the day I go to IGN for my game reviews is the day I lose credibility in myself. Why? Because they are sellouts, duh. But that's neither here nor there.

In the cutscene, you, the MC (main character), have to press F on your keyboard to pay your respects at a funeral. 9GAG, Reddit, Twitter, and other gaming social platforms picked on this meme. But it is on Twitch that you shall see this phrase most commonly.

Among some of the most prominent personalities to use it is PewDiePie, a YouTuber with over 100 Million subscribers.

This brings us to gamer slang, a most prominent user-base of which are teenagers and young-adults. Or, rather, Gen-Z.

Here I would like to draw a comparison. The millennials and Gen-X'ers were known as the generation who were raised by the Boob Tube. Cautionary phrases such as "Stare at the screen too long and you'll rot your brain," were not uncommon for any of us. Yes, sure, some of us had uber-chill parents who were completely fine with the fact that their kids watched TV, but the predominant notion of that time was that TV was a brainless addiction. I can, with complete confidence, say that this whole thing was propagated by the Baby Boomers.

Derogatory phrases that accentuated the importance of the struggle of the Boomers and downplayed the issues of subsequent generations had become far too common in that climate. A toxic aura of ageism mixed with generation bias perpetuated the deepening of the crevice that we know now as the generational gap.

Enter William Higginbotham, a physicist, who in 1958 created the first videogame, Tennis for Two. After reading the instruction manual of the Donner Model 30 Analog Computer, William came to the realization that the Model 30 could calculate the ballistic trajectories of bouncing balls. He took that theory and put it into practice using an oscilloscope. Now, folks, this wasn't something cutting-edge like the Tennis game in GTA V, but it sure was the spiritual predecessor of the whole process.

Once the commercialization of electronics gained terminal velocity, companies such as Atari and Nintendo and Sega made an appearance. Sony got into the game with their PS1. Microsoft decided they'd not be left behind and released the Xbox. Nintendo at that time had a lot of skin in the videogame console game. It had a Color TV-game back in the late '70s, and then evolved from there and released the NES, the SNES, the Nintendo 64, and the GameCube. This didn't happen in a single day, much like the evolution of language into what it is now didn't happen instantly. It took time.

When gamers started discovering that there were other gamers like them all over the globe, gamer slang became a necessity.

Terms like GG became common in multiplayers such as Counterstrike and DOTA. *GG, for example, stands for good game. The term GG can also be used in tandem with WP (well played) in a concatenation called GGWP.*

More terms like these include the word "noob," which stands for newbie, which is derived from new boy, a phrase that the British Army use for recruits.

Now, everyone knows that when a noob gets pwned, you get a GGWP by your clan, because you totally fragged the hell out of a complete scrub, a beta-wannabe-geek with zero skills, forcing him to *DC*.

Take this sentence and throw it casually in front of an unsuspecting boomer (no offense), and watch them convey their confusion to you, followed by asking you if you're okay and are you sure you're not tripping on bath salts?

Other famous terms that are ever-so-popular are AFK (away from keyboard), MIA (missing in action), KS (kill steal), camping (when someone permanently hides in a spot and stays there, taking a lot of advantage in killing other players in the game), glitching (this one's a little too obvious, isn't it?), modding (for when you modify a game), farming, and grinding. The last two refer to when a player decides to become OP (over-powered) by playing through a particular portion of the game over and over. I'll take an example out of a popular RPG (role playing game) called Bloodborne, in which you have to repeatedly grind until your level's just about right to go deal with the boss. And I'm using the example of Bloodborne because it's an insanely popular game of the Soulsborne genre, characterized by its brutal difficulty and its real-time strategy-based gameplay that's labelled by even the most hardcore gamers to be ruthless and terrifying. To defeat the first boss, if you've decided not to use the internet as a crutch to help your first playthrough, you must level up and die repeatedly, then you face the Cleric Beast on the Great Bridge of Central Yharnam.

What's so appealing about Bloodborne anyway? Well, if you earn enough trophies in the game and finish the playthroughs, you get bragging rights and internet points. Points that are useless IRL (in real life), but you can flex (show off) online and form some lifelong bonds. I'm talking ride or die levels of friendship. At the same time, one can argue that it's a bit of a "weird flex but ok" moment. Other than the community, no one probably cares about the fact that you finished Bloodborne multiple times. *'Weird flex but ok' here means something that you think might be worth showing off, but actually isn't as cool as you think it is.*

There's nothing new about Bloodborne. Dungeon crawlers have been around for as long as contemporary video games have been around. The early adapters of the late '90s and early 2000s remember games like Quake and Doom and Duke Nukem and RuneScape. Those games were difficult, yes, and had a fan following that was huge enough that it paved the way to a whole new generation of games built on that premise.

My point in this long tangent? Evolution.

If my info-dump has exhausted you mentally, you may rest by a bonfire, which is another term taken from Dark Souls and Bloodborne. This term meaning a literal bonfire where you can rest and replenish your energy without the fear of any bosses and unsolicited enemies bothering you. If you browse the endless scroll of Reddit and Facebook deep enough, you'll come across posts where someone's posted a picture of a Soulsborne bonfire/lamp, and is asking you to rest before you continue your digital quest.

Since we're so deep in this whole extemporaneous history lesson, I'll now mention digital content creators who are in large part responsible for the propagation of Gen-Z slang.

On the 14th of February, 2005, the video-sharing platform that is now a 15-billion-dollar-a-year business, was developed by three nerds Steve Chen, Chad Hurley, and Jawed Karim. This paved the way for the first generation of YouTubers, who are not only integral in creating Gen-Z slang, but also one of the most frequent users of it.

Smosh, an internet sketch group by duo Ian Hecox and Anthony Padilla formed in 2002, was one of the earliest adopters of YouTube. Their channel has more than 25 million subscribers today and uploads content regularly.

A timeline of first-gen YouTubers shows that PewDiePie (belovingly called Pewds by his fans), who made his own debut on YouTube in April 2010 and rose to fame for his gaming playthrough videos and his lowkey, boy-next-door, edgy comedy, surpassed Smosh as the most subscribed channel on the 15th of August, 2013. Following his footprints, Jacksepticeye and Markiplier rose to a similar fame, utilizing the same formula: gaming playthroughs with their reactions recorded in real-time.

And Smosh had a gaming channel of their own, where they did pretty much the same thing.

This trend caught so much fire that bigtime corporations like Disney started taking notice.

Whatever these titans of content creating industry said became law. All right, maybe I'm being a bit too dramatic over here, but there's no denying that these first-gen YouTubers were also some of the first-gen Influencers.

With numbers on their side, they set the trend for video games. The most amazing part about their rise to fame was that it was mostly, largely, seemingly organic. Smosh weren't some bigtime firm trying to tear a chunk off the internet for themselves. They were just two idiotic, slaphappy boys making funny videos. Pewds was a dropout and was doing odd jobs

while making these videos that'd over ten years
ensure his YouTube throne, if you don't count T-
Series (an Indian music channel that has the most
subs on the platform).

Phrases like 9-year-olds, 19-year-olds, pro-gamers,
epic gamer move, meme review are in common
usage by PewDiePie's fanbase, thus perpetuating this
slang amongst an international community, forming
the language of a new subculture. This subculture
communicated with other alternate cultures of the
21st century, and after this weird mashup, you have
the Gen-Z lingo. Mr. Beast, an American YouTuber
with more than 60 million subscribers for his
wholesome and family-friendly content centering
around donations, wild contests, and exorbitant
amounts of money trading hands, is another important character in this language. Like other famous
YouTubers, he too has been a massive gamer and has
catered to that demographic by giving away consoles
in his videos.

A vast majority of these YouTubers have their own
groups, pages, subreddits, and communities, where
their fans post online content constantly. For example,   PewDiePie   has   a   subreddit   called
r/pewdiepiesubmissions, which has around 3.5

million members. For an individual creator, that's a large fan following.

With all of that stated, my conclusion for this chapter would be: Gen-Z slang has major roots in gaming culture, which in turn has its roots in its own community, a community that has expanded online and has given traditional media a run for its money. Gaming as of right now is estimated to be a $256.97 billion industry by 2025.

When lead characters in multibillion dollar franchises like Avengers use Fortnite references in the largest grossing movie of all time (Avengers: Endgame), you know that gaming slang is not only here to stay but has also deeply rooted itself in the Gen-Z crowd, almost indistinguishably, because if you are Gen-Z, there's a good chance you're an avid gamer, regardless of whether you're doing it on your phone, your consoles, or your PC, and if you're playing games, you're using the language, and you're in most of the inside jokes, if not all.

Tech billionaires like Elon Musk cater to the younger demographic by communicating in Gen-Z slang. Seriously. Check it out. You'll either think of it as the most hilarious thing on the entire planet or you'll say, "Poor Musk, he's got a classic case of the

Peter Pan Syndrome." Regardless, he's an icon amongst the Gen-Z. If he has his way, Gen-Z will be the one of the first people to settle on Mars. Maybe the whole slang will evolve into what shall years from now be known as Mars slang. One can only hope.

In a crossover episode of Meme Review, Elon Musk and Justin Roiland (the co-creator of Rick and Morty) reviewed memes, as requested by PewDiePie, and that too became viral meme material that's still being utilized to this day. The meme template of Musk laughing at the meme of a dead deer under-water is still in popular use.

To try to make sense of Gen-Z slang and its origins is going to sound like a very futile attempt, considering how sporadic, how impromptu, how arbitrary, and how volatile the origin of these phrases are. But I hope my documentation of recent gaming history and its connection to some popular slangs made some sense of the complex language our younger generation is using these days to communicate with each other.

4

INITIATE DECRYPTING SEQUENCE (PT.1)

You've been very patient, humoring me as I shared my findings with you. Now, we shall decrypt their language. Reverse engineer it so that it's accessible to us as well. Without further ado, here is an inclusive list of the most used slang among the Gen-Z.

1. Basic

Basic essentially means anything that's mainstream. It can be used to describe a person who loves mainstream things and thus is a very unoriginal specimen of the human species.

Examples of this word are: "Yeah, that dude only posts The Office memes on his timeline. Pretty basic stuff. And yeah, his favorite singer? Guess who. Taylor Swift. That's basic, yo."

If you like The Office. You're basic. However, if you like The Good Place by the same guy (Mike Schur), you're woke.

If your favorite writing by Edgar Allan Poe is "The Raven," you're basic. If your favorite piece of writing by Mr. Poe is, I don't know, Berenice, then you're in the clear.

If you love Fortnite, you're basic. However, if your favorite first-person-shooter is some indie game that no one's heard of, such as Syndicate, you're cool.

Basic is Gen-Z's way of declaring someone uncool. Some linguistic experts and scholars of the Gen-Z behavior suggest that the very act of calling something basic *is* basic.

2. Based

A based person is someone who is true to themselves. They don't care about the popular opinion or what's trending or what's largely accepted as the norm. They speak their mind; they say the unpopular opinion out loud.

Example? Sure. "That chick's crazy based. Even though her entire family voted for Obama twice and then once again for Biden, she wears her MAGA hat and listens to Kanye's raps."

In this scenario, it's implied that the girl, because she's chosen to go against the Democratic norm of her house and has declared her support for the Republicans, namely Trump and Kanye, she's based.

More uses of this terminology are easily found online wherein someone on Facebook or Reddit posts a really unpopular opinion that, get this, is actually quite a popular opinion but people are too afraid to voice it out loud.

3. Big yikes

It's just yikes, but bigger, as the well thought out term implies. It is used when something extremely shocking, disturbing, embarrassing, or peculiar happens.

A use case for this term would be, "Ey, so dad caught me watching hentai, and he confronted me about it. Big yikes, my guys."

Here, the subject was apprehended by their father for watching Japanese cartoon porn. As a result, they were most likely apprehended, scolded, or reprimanded. Later, in a meeting with a friend, they exhibited their getting caught with the expression "big yikes."

4. Bop

This is an easy one. Bop refers to a good song or a nice beat. When someone wishes to use brevity when describing a good song, they use the word bop.

"Hey, that Bebe Rexha single straight up bops."

"The latest Eminem diss track is a bop."

Bop originates from the 1940s fast-tempo jazz *bebop*. It is an imitative term, as in it is the sound that your hands make when you bop something.

5. Canceled

Ooh. The term canceled drives fear in the hearts of pre-established boomers and Gen-X'ers all over the world. What does it mean? It means to stop supporting a person or a cause by following a series of steps, such as unfollowing them on social media, posting exposés about them online, boycotting, and using specific hashtags to get a movement going.

Usage: "After we heard that Kevin Spacey had sexually assaulted a child back when he was in his twenties (Kevin Spacey, not the child), we've decided to cancel him."

And cancel him they did. Spacey's hit Netflix drama House of Cards is a classic example of that. Once enough people had gotten behind the cause of cancelling him, the execs at Netflix removed him from the main role. The show ended a season later as well with terrible ratings.

While it's a largely positive movement meant to call out those in authority for their wrongdoings, there's an element of censorship to the whole cancel culture. Todd Phillips, the director of the Hangover movies, said, in an interview with Vanity Fair, that he left making comedy movies like Road Trip and Old School because of this woke culture spreading around.

"Go try to be funny nowadays with this woke culture," Phillips said. "There were articles written about why comedies don't work anymore—I'll tell you why, because all the fucking funny guys are like, 'Fuck this shit, because I don't want to offend you.'"

Joker did end up grossing around 1.074 billion dollars at the box office, and Joaquin Phoenix did end up winning the Academy Award for Best Actor in a Leading Role.

Maybe it's not entirely a lost cause, there, Mr. Phillips?

6. Cap

Cap means lie, and not just any lie. It's not a white lie, it's not something harmless. It's a straight up, blatant lie.

It isn't used as much on its own. The most common term you'll find cap being used in is, "no cap."

For example, "I just finished my first playthrough of the latest Mario game, and no cap, my guy, that game is trash."

You can combine no cap with other popular Gen-Z phrases and make a very complex sentence, like so, "No cap, my dude, but Ariana Grande's latest collaboration with Kesha was bopping, but I don't get why it got canceled on Twitter. Big yikes, am I right? All these basic peeps are dragging on our queen, which is so not based."

In African-American slang, to cap means to brag about something. As with many Gen-Z terms that are popular these days, this term itself dates to the early 1900s.

7. Catch these hands

When someone says "catch these hands," you better stand back or retreat, because this is a call to arms. You don't want to catch someone's hands. This term is a confrontational one, meant to incite a fight between two parties.

"If you think that the latest Mario game is trash, you better get out of my way, because you so don't want to catch these hands. Nintendo can't do nothing wrong!"

"Keep talking smack about my boy and you'll be catching these hands!"

Its origins can be traced to Braun Strowman, a WWE wrestler, who used this catchphrase. "Get these hands" means the same thing as well. However,

Mr. Strowman argued that he wasn't the coiner of these terms.

8. Drag

A drag is a roast. It's a confrontational diss. It means to make fun of something, to criticize something, or to tear something to shreds with your words.

"She was dragging me so hard today for wearing those apple bottom jeans and boots with the fur. I just wanted to bring back the late 2000s, man, what's so wrong with that?"

In whomever was dragging you for sporting apple bottom jeans and boots with the fur's defense, if you're trying to bring back something in style, why something from the early 2000s? There are so many better eras to get inspiration from.

9. Drip

Drip is a nice sense of style. It defines sartorial coolness. Drip is the way someone carry themselves. Drip is a nice combo of Levi's jeans, a Supreme sweatshirt, and PlayStation themed Nikes, I'm assuming.

"Nicole's drip was fire. It was class. She was an icon. It made me feel jealous, you know?"

10. Fam

Fam is a term everyone can understand. It connotes to someone in your inner circle, a person you've bonded with. A gender-neutral term, fam is used to emphasize love and closeness with a particular person.

"She's my fam. She gets me. When I got cancelled on Twitter last week for saying that the Mario game wasn't trash, she joined me on Zoom and dragged everybody and warned them to back off or catch these hands. I love her. Everyone needs a fam like that."

As much as we'd all love to discuss more of these slangs, it's time to move on and come back to the decryption booth later. Now we'll look at names that have become memes.

5

WHEN YOUR NAME BECOMES A MEME

Elon Musk, the gift that keeps on giving, named his baby X Æ A-12. Before you break your brain, like I did in attempts to try to pronounce the name, I'll tell you how to say it: "X Ash A Twelve." There.

No. I'm sorry. That still does not take away the strangeness of the name. Musk said that the name was inspired from the Archangel-12 plane. His girl-friend Grimes stated that X was the unknown vari-able, the Æ was her elven spelling of AI which could either mean love or Artificial Intelligence, and the A-12 was the precursor to SR-17, which was her and Musk's favorite aircraft. It had no weapons, no defenses, and only had speed. And another A stands for Archangel, which is her favorite song.

Yes, the name became an instant meme, sketches were made on YouTube, people took to social media and a few concerned parents reached out on Twitter to Grimes and Musk and shared their thoughts about how the name could be used in the future to bully the boy in school and online.

That's just one of the many names that have become memes, or memefied, for lack of a better term.

On a more specific note, let's talk about Karen and Keith and Sharon and Chad and Kyle. First off, let's all collectively apologize to the holders of these names. We didn't know that they'd become memes. None of us did. That's the power of memes. No one knows what's gonna go viral one minute, no one knows what's going to stick. That's both beautiful and scary.

The assumption about the name Karen goes like this: She's cranky, privileged, hateful, arrogant, and always demands to speak to the manager of an institution because she believes she's been wronged somehow by the staff there. Her entitlement knows no bounds. She's either a trophy wife or a middle-aged woman who has nothing better to do in her time than boast about her kids, rant about politics, express her dissatisfaction with everything ranging from violent video games to bold lyrics of rap songs. She tries to mask her racism but it shows. She tries to make virtue signaling statements about "back in my day" even though she's no older than forty. Her utopia is where everyone acknowledges that she is the queen, and all the people are posh white people sitting in the foyer and drinking iced teas and talking about the latest developments at the PTA meeting at the private school that teaches French as a mandatory language.

It's a stereotype that's surfaced because of viral videos in which women of a certain demographic were seen misbehaving with staff, showing off their privilege card, and being nuisances to an otherwise normal society.

Nowadays, whenever anyone uses the term Karen online, it's meant to be used in a derogatory fashion.

Similarly, Sharon and Susan and Sandra are names that have become the butt of jokes in recent years, the most common stereotype being that they're names of annoying women, whether in the form of aunts, colleagues, or people you accidentally come across in real life.

One of the most common terms you've used is "Bye Felicia." It originates from the hilarious film Friday, starring Ice Cube and Chris Tucker.

Whenever someone announces their departure from a Facebook group in a very self-righteous farewell post about how the group has gone to the dogs, people post the "Bye Felicia" gif or meme in the comments, followed by the "This is a Facebook group, not a Departure Lounge, so no need to announce that you're leaving" variety of comments.

One can argue that 'Bye Felicia' is where all of this started, but no one can know for sure. It's for the internet gods to decide.

Other names that have garnered hate are Jan, Kyle, and Chad.

Chads are members of the male species who are pure alphas. Everything they do is the symbolic representation of a strong male persona in the 21st century. The name is used in an ironic capacity.

Similarly, Jan. Jan is a person who always lies. Not a single utterance of truth can come from the contorted lips of a person who bears the name of Jan.

A Harold is a person who's too old and stupid to understand anything of significance. The name Harold is the predecessor to the viral term Boomer. Before there was "Ok Boomer," there was Harold. You could focus all of your hate and concentrate into one word. Harold.

Using names as the punchlines for jokes has become increasingly common in recent years. The format of these jokes is very generic:

Person A describes Person B doing something banal or irritating or boring or stupid.

Person B is the butt of the joke.

Person A finishes the joke by doing an angry-outburst routine concatenated with Person B's name.

Example:

> "So last week my neighbor decided he wanted his dog to sniff my dog's ass in public, right as I was welcoming guests over to my place. Oh, please, Simon, don't mind me greeting the head of research of my university's Comp. Sci department into my home. Please, let your chihuahua shove her nose up my unsuspecting

Timmy's asshole. It's perfectly normal. Thanks Simon."

Now this name will become a shorthand, and a cultural one at that, for similar behavior that other people observed in their vicinity. Now every annoying neighbor who does something embarrassing in public can be termed a Simon.

Another way names become viral for their funny-factor is movies. The whole "My name is Jeff" craze immortalized the name Jeff as a brainless classic joke. Now every Jeff has a default joke in their chamber. A timeless "My name is Jeff" in response to anything. In my opinion, that's just cheating.

Deborah Cameron, a feminist linguist and professor of Language and Communication at Oxford University, said, "Names give social information." She further went to theorize: "I'm guessing these particular names have been chosen to say 'middle aged (and possible lower middle-class) white woman'. Perhaps this type of woman is considered an acceptable butt for jokes about annoying women because she's 'generic', there's no race or class angle."

Kyle has become a very infamous internet archetype. A typical Kyle drinks a ton of Monster, slams his first into drywall every chance he can get, wears sleeveless shirts that are also ripped and in poor taste, possibly belonging to his father who ran off to buy e-cigarettes when Kyle was still young.

Kyle loves monster trucks, playing GTA V, and has no plans about the future. Kyle is also sometimes a fuckboy, trying to appeal to women beyond his league through his odd trinkets, catchphrases, and very basic taste in music and beverages.

> I hope Kyle grows out of it, gets a job as a forensic analyst, settles down, and stops drinking Monster. They wreck your teeth, Kyle. It's not even funny. Please, hydrate on plain water. Drink some lemon tea. Cut your sugar intake. Stop smoking that weird blueberry vape. We care about you.
>
> — THE REST OF THE WORLD NOT NAMED
> KYLE

Again, as with every other thing that Gen-Z does, there's nothing new about this.

Remember the Sex and the City craze where everyone was labelling each other as a Samantha or a

Miranda or a Carrie or a Charlotte? Yeah, it's pretty much that with less accessible characters.

It means nothing. It's like saying you're a such a Virgo because you always Keto in March and then do a detox in January. You're assigning character traits to names, star signs, pop-culture icons, and movie, videogame, and film characters. And yet, culturally speaking, it means everything to Gen-Z, like back in the day when we said someone was such a Kramer or a Costanza or an Elaine.

Man, I miss Seinfeld.

6

DTF OR DTR? GEN-Z DATING SLANG

The oldest Gen-Z is 24 years old as of 2021. That means there's a ton of them out there, dating.

Not to come off as a creep interested in the sex-lives of those who're way younger than me, but if I'm decoding the whole Gen-Z slang, then I must also understand how they're communicating with each other in the dating department.

Before we go further, we must understand that most Gen-Z people opened their eyes in a world where internet dating wasn't so much of a stigma anymore than it was the norm. Ok Cupid, J-Date, and all these other websites paved the way for apps. Now you have Tinder, Grindr, Bumble, Happn, and dozens of themed dating apps that you can use to discover more people.

Here are some buzzwords and slang terms that I discovered in my quest to absorb this new language. Of course, some of them aren't new at all.

1. **Aromantic**

Aromantic describes someone who doesn't conform to the whole romantic part of the relationship. We've been made to feel like love and marriage are the predetermined norm. However, aromantics are not only challenging the status quo, but also redefining it. One can comment that it is sexual hedonism wearing a glamorous dress, but one can be wrong, as it's quickly becoming a very common term.

2. **Asexual**

Somewhat quite the opposite of aromantic, asexuals feel romantic feelings toward their partners but either can't or don't want to participate in the sexual aspects of the relationship because of having no feelings below their navels. It's an actual sexuality in the spectrum.

3. Benching

Benching is when you like someone but don't actually want to commit to them long-term, but are also not sure if you want to move on from them because there's no better option available right now. The term comes from sports, from when they bench you until the coach needs you. Gotta be honest, this one's a little disturbing.

4. Big dick energy

Big dick energy refers to the charisma, the macho, the confidence that a person emanates as a result of their having a metaphorical large phallus. It doesn't depend on the size of your penis. It's got to do with your charisma. You can have a micropenis and rock big dick energy. You can be a lesbian and still emanate big dick energy.

5. Breadcrumbing

When you like someone but not enough to commit to them, you send them leading flirty messages that are ambiguous in nature and lack the element of confrontationality.

6. Catfishing/Wokefishing

Catfishing is when you're pretending to be someone online whom you're not. Woke-fishing is the same as catfishing, wherein you pretend that you have woke thoughts and beliefs whereas in truth you don't. Basically being a hypocrite online to get laid.

7. Cuffing season

The etymology of cuffing season comes from African American Vernacular English, and implies cuffing yourself to someone willingly for a specific period, i.e., between early fall and late winter.

8. Curve

If you get curved, it means you're rejected.

9. Cushioning

If you keep in touch with more than one potential romantic partner, you're cushioning, especially if you're not certain about how things are going to go with your main squeeze.

10. **Daddy**

Daddy is your boyfriend, your boo, your bae, your casual partner if they emanate a fatherly aura. Yeah, the term is incestuous in nature and would give one Mr. Freud a field day were he alive today.

11. **Demisexual**

Someone who identifies sexually as only being attracted to other people based on emotional computability.

12. **DM Sliding**

When you direct message your crush on social media, you're sliding into their direct messages.

14. **DTR Convo**

A pivotal movement in the relationship, the DTR convo is an important talk you need to have to "define the relationship."

15. **Eggplant Emoji**

This just means penis.

16. Emergency call

When you're on the risk of going on a bad date, you tell one of your friends to give you an emergency call to cop you out of the terrible date.

17. Firedooring

Textbook definition of a one-sided relationship in which someone, an introvert in most of these cases, goes way out of their way to text you but when you start talking to them, they don't reciprocate equally. It's irritating. It's called firedooring.

18. Freckling

Like cuffing season, freckling is when people appear in warm months to date you. Maybe it's because they got out of a relationship and want a quick fling or something of the sort. When summer ends, they'll ditch you.

19. FWB (Friends with benefits)

When you and your "friend" decide to share all the benefits of the relationship with each other but don't go on and commit to each other. It became quite the mainstream term when Mila Kunis and Justin Timberlake made the movie with the same name.

20. Fuckbuddies

While friends with benefits is a classy term, fuck-buddies is the same relationship arrangement without the hassle of sugarcoating it.

21. Ghosting

Ghosting is when you decide to disappear from a person's life with little to no explanation.

22. Haunting

As the name implies, its when your ex starts stalking your social media, leaving a trail of likes in the wake of their haunting.

23. Incel

A portmanteau of involuntary and celibate, an incel is someone who doesn't get laid, but not by choice. It implies someone is so unpopular and unappealing that people don't want to be with them, let alone sleep with them.

24. **Kittenfishing**

Kittenfishing is virtue-signaling and appearing self-righteous on dating apps. It's dishonest, it's rude, it's borderline catfishing. The difference? In catfishing you take on a different persona entirely. In kitten-fishing, you lie a lowkey lie. If you're a first-year med student, you'll put doctor in your profile bio. Stuff like that.

25. **Left on read/seen**

The worst thing you can do to someone is to leave them on read or seen in a messaging app. It's a blow to the other person's ego.

26. **Lockering**

If someone ditches you because "they're studying", you've been lockered.

27. **Love bombing**

Sometimes a person puts in way too much effort at the start of the relationship and doesn't follow it through. The earlier effort is there to make the person being love bombed feel special and nice. It's manipulative and abusive, this technique.

28. **Microcheating**

Oftentimes a person in a relationship may cheat on another person on a very miniscule level. That is called microcheating. It involves sending someone some flirty texts, maybe sending some lewd images of yourself, reacting to their provocative photography, and so on.

29. **Phubbing**

Folks, it is as gross a term as it sounds. Phubbing here means going out on a date with someone, and then observing your partner constantly staring at their phone.

30. **Pie hunting**

Pies here refer to people who're emotionally broken. A pie hunter is someone who seeks out broken people on purpose, people with messy dating histories, to take advantage of them.

31. **Redpill**

Taken from the Matrix, this term implies that you're a man who has realized that women are being treated very specially by society and so you have become so woke you realize that and hate this bias and thus are going to stay away from women.

32. **Roaching**

Hiding the fact that you're dating around from a new partner so as to give them a sense of exclusivity is roaching.

33. **Sapiosexual**

A person attracted solely to intelligence in their partner.

34. **Several-night-stand**

There's no commitment, but there's an agreement that you and your partner shall sleep around for a given number of nights, then move on.

35. Sex interview

Having sex before deciding to be in a relationship with someone to gauge sexual compatibility is called a sex interview.

36. Situationship

It's not a friendship, it's not a relationship, it's something in between. It's a situationship.

37. Slow fade

This one's hilarious. When you feel like your relationship is dying, instead of ghosting the other person, you decide to "slow fade" the relationship, reducing contact slowly, being less and less intimate, and then one day, boom, it's not there anymore.

38. Snack

A person who's delectable in appearance. A gorgeous babe, a honey, a smokeshow, a stunner. That's what a snack is.

39. Stashing

In stashing, you hide your partner (stash 'em away) from the public to avoid confrontation with your peers and family members so that you can avoid the whole commitment talk with anyone.

40. Stealthing

When a guy removes a condom during sexual intercourse, it's pronounced stealthing.

41. Submarining

When a toxic person keeps making cameos in your life after breaking up with you, dipping in and out of existence, that's submarining.

42. Swiping

Easy. Swiping on Bumble and Tinder implies liking someone so much that you swiped right on them or abhorring someone so much that you swiped left on them.

43. **Textlationship**

A relationship strictly existing in text messages. It never seems to manifest in real life.

44. **Thirst trap**

When someone posts provocative pictures and content online, they're laying down a thirst trap.

45. **Throning**

It's essentially gold-digging but with a little pizzazz. You use someone for their power or social status or money, ergo vying for the throne.

46. **Tindstagramming**

Some profiles on Tinder have Instagram links in the bio. When a person uses Tinder to find Instagram IDs of people, that's called Tindstagramming.

47. **Turkey dump**

A college student, when they return home for Thanksgiving, realize that they can't keep things going with their long-distance partner, and break up on Thanksgiving. The Turkey Dump. Patent pending.

48. Uncuffing season

When you break up with your partner in springtime after cuffing with them earlier on.

49. Vulturing

When you realize that the relationship is dying out like a star, you start being very selfish with your partner. That's called vulturing.

50. Water droplets emoji

This emoji means ejaculate/semen/vaginal fluids. Basically sexy fluids.

51. Zombieing

When you ghost someone for so long that you're considered dead and then you show up after a certain number of days, that's when you're being a zombie.

You must either be feeling wildly intrigued or completely grossed out after discovering these phrases. The fact of the matter is, these terms are here to stay and evolve. There's nothing we can do about it other than adapt. Bob Dylan said it true when he said, "Times, they are a 'changing." For more hot-off-the-press references like that, stay tuned for the next chapter.

Ooh, DTF. DTF means down to fuck.

7

RESUME DECRYPTING SEQUENCE (PT.2)

Where were we? At fam, right? Okay, let's continue decrypting the Gen-Z lingo.

1. Finesse

When you want to get something but can't do so by ordinary means, you finesse it. You trick someone, you hoodwink them, manipulate, and bamboozle the hell out of them. Yes. That's the way it goes.

Example? Sure. "Mom and dad were being real babies about spending a bunch of their hard-earned money on that Mario game, the one everyone's been criticizing lately, and so I had to finesse them out of just about enough money to get the game for me and my fam."

Another example: "Being a millennial parent is so hard. Just yesterday my daughter finessed me out of a few dollars. She thinks I don't know it's for that stupid Mario game. When is she going to grow up and play some Zelda like a grown-up person?"

2. Glow up

There are times in the lifespan of a Gen-Z person when they go through a phase of spiritual, mental, or physical change. We used to call it spiritual rezoning back at our Laser Lotus Buddha Cult. They call it Glow up.

Example: "Bethany went to Tahiti with her mom's new boyfriend and found a shaman there. She had a major glow up and came back with dreadlocks and ancient Eastern wisdom."

Good for you, Bethany.

3. High key

The opposite of low key, high key is a synonym for "very" or "really" or "a lot."

Example: "Even though I high key believe that Bethany's glow up has really changed her for the better, but low key, though, I know she's just trying to finesse everybody into believing that she's born again as a good girl just to get her hands on that god-awful Mario game."

I should clarify here, folks, I'm not being paid by Nintendo. It's just that I'm way too deep with that Mario joke, and I can't go back. I can't go back. Someone help me find a more fitting reference.

4. Hits different

When something stands out from the rest, it makes you feel special. It makes you feel different from other things. It hits different.

"Yo, after her glow up, everything Bethany says hits different. I used to really hate that Mario game, but now it just hits different when I play it as a metaphor for man's eternal struggle to push that Sisyphus rock of societal difficulties up the slope of adversities. It just hits different."

5. I'm dead

Imagine you're a parent in their mid-forties and your child is sitting in the next room and then suddenly yells out, "I'm dead!" Your paternal instincts activate, you start seeing red, Terminator vision full-flared, you don your leather jacket and your sunglasses and take that shotgun out from under the sofa where you'd stowed it for emergencies. It's time to rescue your child.

When you go in the next room, you find them rolling on the floor, laughing, clutching their stomach, their eyes glued to their phone's screen.

"My child, what's wrong?"

"Dad, I'm dead."

"But my heir, the fruit of my loins, you are clearly alive and breathing. All vital systems are operating optimally."

"Dad. Look at this meme. Pepe the frog is yeeting and skeeting to Lil Pump. I'm dead."

It dawns on you. They find it hilarious and are deploying hyperbole of the nth order to express their glee. Your finger twitches on the shotgun trigger. Your grandad fought in WWII for this. A single patriotic tear rolls down your eye. Freedom comes at a cost.

7. MC (Main Character)

Back in the good old days, things didn't have as many labels attached to them. When you picked up a Neil Gaiman novel, you knew it was a fantasy novel. You were blissfully unaware of the whole subgenre web of lies that marketers used.

Not so much anymore. Everyone knows everything in this age of freedom of information. What was once a shorthand used by screenwriters and other members of the literary arts is now reduced to someone who's an extrovert, charismatic, and is the leader of their group. The main character, in other words.

"Stacy's such an MC of the whole Lisbon Falls High Sophomore Clan. She's the director of her season, the main cast, the producer, and she's...omg I'm secretly in love with Stacy."

8. Periodt

To emphasize a point being made, but with more emphasis on the emphasis, the term periodt was fashioned deep in the forges of Mordor. It's so revolutionary, Oxford has declared it the single-most important contribution to language since the invention of the word queef.

"This Pewds music video about Hades bops —periodt."

At this point, I'm nearing giving up. But I must press on.

9. Pressed

When you're mad or upset about something, such as I am about where language is headed, you're pressed.

"Stacy was pressed because Bethany's glow up straight up stole Stacy's limelight. Everyone's forgotten about the Mario game now that Stacy is pressed."

10. Sis

Sis affectionately means sister—no muscles pulled there—and is used for a close friend.

"Stacy is my sis, and so is Bethany, but you're my sis too, Frankie, so now I'm really pressed about what to do about all of this. I just wanted to low-key play my Mario game, the one everyone's talking about —periodt."

11. Sending me

A person finds something funny and they can't use "I'm dead" because their little brother just used that term and made their dad don his Terminator costume, so they use "Sending me" instead.

"My lil bro reacted to the fire meme I sent him and said "I'm dead" and my dad got mad. Sending me rn (right now). Sending so much me. Omg. F's in the chat for boomers."

12. Slaps

Similar to bop, slaps is also an adjective that describes how amazing something is.

"That MC Slap song about slapping slappers really slaps, on God, no cap. It's an entire bop unto its own."

13. **Snatched**

Imagine with me a little here, folks. Say you're walking down your favorite boulevard, wearing a nice t-shirt that you got from Banana Republic, and a nice trouser sort of thing that your cousin from Europe sent you because it's the latest fashion in Prague, and you're just minding your business, walking and walking and walking, and then someone says out of the blue," Hey, your dressage is utter snatched, my dude."

You look around, startled. Who is this rapscallion taking your clothes off here in public? Do thieves have no morals anymore? There was a time when every crook followed the code. Now look where things are, someone's snatching your clothes. Truly, the decline of Western civilization is nigh.

And then someone explains it to you that snatched means an outfit or an ensemble (or anything really) that looks splendid. You relax. The Western civilization still stands. The beacons of hope are still lit.

13. **Stan**

The origin of Stan is from Eminem's song by the same name. It means someone who's a super fan of something, bordering on excessively enthusiastic, especially in case of a celebrity.

"Omg, did you see Stacy's latest Instagram exposé on the exploitation of Tahitian shamans? I stan Stacy so much, no cap. I stan her very hard. Also, Bethany is so canceled."

14. Sus

This term, if I'm correct, originated from that weird game that everyone's been playing this past year. Among us. Sus means suspicious. The end. There's nothing more to it.

"He acts so sus it's like he's hiding something," one might say. Or, "I'm a bit of a detective and I think that Stacy's whole exposé is totes sus, you know? She's just jealous of Bethany."

15. Tea

Tea is code for drama and gossip and slander. You dish tea when you've got some amazing gossip to discuss with your fam.

"So here's the tea, sis. It's like, so, yeah, I was talking to Bethany, and she told me that Stacy's really sus behavior about the whole exposé that she wrote about Tahitian shamans is just low key plagiarized from Vox news's archives. We're cancelling Stacy now. Hashtag unsubscribe."

16. **Vibe**

When New Agers gave birth to their children (no offense), they taught them the term vibe before those children knew how to walk. And so now, even though vibes are pretty much pseudoscientific phenomena that are about as real as Dragon Ball Z's Kamehameha waves, the term is a popular one for describing the aura of someone, their mood, their charisma, and their energy.

"Bethany has such a vibe, she's an entire mood, no cap. And Stacy, well, I heard that Stacy uploaded her apology video on YouTube and it made it to Trending, so now everything's fine and she and Bethany are recording a new video announcing their makeup line. It's such a great year. I love the vibe everyone's giving off."

17. **Wig**

Wig, as in yours got blown off your head when you were exposed to something that was so sheerly awesome that there were no words left in the dictionary to define that level of awesomeness other than the expression for fake hair.

"Eminem's latest diss track of Stacy and Bethany's makeup line, bruh! Wig! Wildin! ISTG! Those girls really went big enough to get dissed by Eminem. Wig times two. Wig times infinity."

18. Yeet

You and I, we have journeyed far in these pages, exploring terms, names, discussing history, dissecting phrases, doing in-depth analysis, expounding upon the frailty of the human condition, hypothesizing about life, asking each other the big questions like "Is there a God?", but now, I must leave you, dear friend. I must bid farewell, and it all starts where it ends.

At yeet, that ambiguous term that means nothing and everything. For all we know it was the first word that's been passed down to us etched on cave walls, noted by the great historians of the Roman Empire, passed down to Western civilization, and immortalized as Gen-Z slang forever and ever.

I must say, old friend, this was a humbling journey.

My faith in humanity, in these pages, was both affirmed and denied. I felt hope writing this, and dread. I laughed. I cried. I remembered the line from the Hindu scripture, the Bhagavad Gita. Vishnu is trying to persuade the Prince that he should do his duty and to impress him takes on his multi-armed form and says, 'now I am become Death, the destroyer of worlds.' I suppose we all thought that one way or another.

And so, I leave you at yeet.

Yeet is a word so powerful that it's an exclamation of your being. It's a call to arms. It's screaming Carpe Diem at the top of your lungs. It's Hakuna Matata. It's the proclamation of existence.

And it also means throwing something with a lot of force.

"Lmao, eyy, did you see me yeet that Mario cartridge off the cliff and record the whole thing and upload it on Nintendo's servers? Yeet!"

It's the perfect mix of brevity and wit, this term. Yeet.

I shall now leave you with one word, hoping against hope that it speaks to you on a spiritual level.

Yeet.

MESSAGE FROM THE AUTHOR

You've reached the end of the book. Thank you so much for reading. I hope this was as helpful to you as much as writing this was fun for me. I hope this experience was informative for you as well.

To help me grow my business, I'd appreciate you leaving a review. I have a fun idea! Why don't you use terms you've learned in this book to write a review for it? Thank you for this, in advance.

If you subscribe to…

Just kidding, there's a bonus chapter waiting for you next! And like most good things in life, it's free. Hint, hint: It's a short story using much of the Gen-Z phrases and terms we've learned in the book. A story for the ages.

BONUS CHAPTER

Hot Girl Bummer - A Gen-Z Short Story

Mr. Wilson's Toyota Corolla was given to him as part of the promotion package last month. He was a diligent man whose hobbies included permaculture, reading about American history, and collecting vintage Americana such as the ship-in-a-bottle owned by Edgar Allan Poe, and Raymond Chandler's bowtie that the famous author used to wear to parties in his old age. It was one of those lazy Sunday afternoons with much sun and little clouds. In short, the perfect time to wash his car.

Mr. Wilson had two children, both of whom were teenagers.

He had a loving wife, a respectable physician at the local hospital.

They lived a good life here in suburban Urbana, except for one not-so-appealing facet: the sudden bandwagon their kids had jumped aboard on, this Gen-Z slang thing. Lately, both Sid and Tara had been speaking a new language that seemed to fly over both Mr. and Mrs. Wilson's heads.

Late at night, when the curtains were drawn and Mrs. Wilson (first name Claire) and Mr. Wilson (first name Ben) were wedged deep in their blanket with only their elbows and heads popping out, they discussed their kids' new language.

"Last night they were singing this song that I didn't understand a single lyric of!" Claire proclaimed defeatedly in bed last night.

"Oh, yeah? What was the name of the song?"

"Hot Girl Bummer!" Claire had yelled.

"That's an innocent-sounding song. Remember us, sweetie, back when we were kids? Remember when

Cher was all the rage and our parents had just about enough of her autotuned voice? Remember that? Back when that was happening, my mom used to say that she was glad she grew up when music made sense. Yeah right, mom. What about The Bee Gees makes sense?" Mr. Wilson said.

"That may be, but this is different, Ben! Look at the lyrics! I looked them up online and they're complete garbled nonsense," Claire said. She was on the verge of tears. "Sid and Tara sing it all day long. Look at the lyrics."

Mr. Wilson had taken a look at his wife's iPad.

The lyrics went like this:

Fuck you, and you, and you
I hate your friends and they hate me too
I'm through, I'm through, I'm through
This that hot girl bummer anthem
Turn it up and throw a tantrum.

He conveyed to his wife that clearly the artist was conveying his angst and it was nothing more. His wife said that the artist could maybe express his angst privately and not ruin her children.

"Hey, dad!" Sid was out on the porch with his Nintendo Switch in one hand, his Dr. Pepper in the other.

"Now, now, Sid, what did I tell you about Dr. Pepper rotting your teeth?" he said, throwing water over his car's windshield.

"Dad, can you maybe tell mom to chill? She deleted the song from my computer, thinking she'd deleted it permanently. I have it on my Spotify. It's also there on YouTube. What's she trying to do?"

"She's just trying to get you to stop listening to the song. She thinks that's a terrible influence on you," he said. "It's coarse, uncouth, and dangerous, she says. What do you think?"

"Dad, me and Tara are just having fun, you know that, right?" Sid said. His little sister, sixteen years of age, came out and punched Sid in the shoulder.

"I know, I know," Mr. Wilson said.

"Dad, did you have your own language back when you were our age?" Tara asked. She was wearing her mom's vintage Beetlejuice t-shirt.

"Well, from what I remember, we used to call everything rad."

"What does rad mean?"

Mrs. Wilson came out with a pitcher of iced tea.

"Honey, the kids want to know what rad means," Bill called out.

"Oh, just let 'em know it means the same thing as tubular," Claire said, putting the tray on the table.

"Yo, Sid, they're lowkey scaring me, no cap, fam," Tara said to her elder brother.

"Word. Them peeps be bopping to some real basic Merriam, ya hear?" Sid said, nodding gravely.

"Bet. Hella big yikes on these boomers. F's in the chat, my guy," Tara agreed.

Mr. and Mrs. Wilson look at each other and talk in that telepathic manner that all couples develop a few years into their marriage.

It's time we taught these kids a lesson, Claire said.

Damn right, Ben replied.

"Sid?" Ben said.

"Yeah, dad?"

"You know how you kids think everything's cool until your parents start using it?"

"We don't think that, dad. We know that," Tara replied for her brother.

"Then prepare to be completely annihilated, because last night me and your father bought a book online and learned ALL of your slang," Claire said, grinning sinisterly.

"Oh, sweet God in heaven, please don't ruin *this* for us," Tara said, true horror etched on her face. Sid sat up, his arms tremoring, his fingers jittering, his eyes bulging.

"Mom. Dad. We'll be nice. We'll have fun with you. We'll go to church every Sunday. Me and Tara won't ever rebel against you two ever again. We'll be the perfect kids. Just stop. Don't go any further. Let this be the one thing that remains ours, please," Sid begged.

Claire and Ben were now standing side-by-side, towering over their petrified kids.

Claire magically made a boombox appear out of thin air. Ben put on his vintage Ray Bans, rolled up his sleeves, unbuttoned his shirt to reveal a gold chain and a white vest underneath, and suddenly, the air became very cool and the sky turned dark.

"This is a rap me and your mom made to drive home the fact that Gen-Z slang isn't as covert as you two think it is," Ben said.

"Drop the beat, papa bear," Claire said.

"Right back at ya, mama bear," Ben clicked on the play button on the boombox.

Tara and Sid grabbed on to each other for dear life.

"You might wanna catch these hands, son," Ben began, perfectly in tune to the beat:

> And yeah,
> I own the rights to call you son,
> seeing as how you're literally my seed.
> Catch you up to speed?
> Un-unh. I'ma drag this like a stag,
> and drip mad fashion like I was Sebastian,
> fam.

Clair went like:

That's right,
Mr. Hubby hub, hub.
These kids be glowing up,
throwing up,
high key thinking they're
being low key,
and not the Odin kind,
never you mind,
you don't even have time to look behind,
so suck on orange rinds
in the bleachers at soccer practice,
or we will teach you a lesson so hard
you'll be dry as a cactus,
believing it hits different
when they speak like this,
well, be prepared to be dissed like this!

Once Ben and Claire had spitted their fire bars, a large crowd had gathered around them. Children, teenagers, old people, young people—everyone was there. People were recording videos on their phones. All of a sudden, this wasn't the quiet front yard of a sleepy suburbia.

Tara and Sid stood up from their seats. Tara put her iPhone in the dock and played her beat. Now it was their turn to defend themselves.

Tara coughed and cleared her throat. People were cheering her parents, but just as she stood up, everyone was quiet except for the blaring beat.

> Yo, word of caution before you listen to these
>> boomers:
> They're lyrical doomers, still believing in
>> WhatsApp rumors,
> we gonna weed 'em out like surgeons do
>> tumors.
> You think you can figure out our slang? I'm
>> dead,
> and that's rhetorical, as in metaphorical,
> you're a washed-up tech like Oracle!
> Periodt. My man Sid on the mike, and his rap
>> slaps,
> and not in the abusive way!

Sid took his dad's Ray Bans from him and put them on. Now he was the cool one being cheered by the crowd.

> Snatch me, you can't catch me,
> if I were an egg, you couldn't hatch me,
> I'm the MC of this story, you're just a
>> stan, man,

We don't buy vans or sedans, man,
because we're environmentally conscious,
and if you wanna spill some tea,
better prepare for a brutal fatality,
because my vibe speaks to my Gen-Z tribe!
We're wigging it, chigging it, licking it,
    sticking it,
saying yeet to these sick beats,
performing lyrical feats that would make
    Biggy proud! Sid out!

The police arrive. They're there to control the rabid crowd. There's a barbecue going in the back. College kids are shirtless and bathing in sprinklers. There are signs in the air, half of them supporting Sid and Tara, while the other half have affirmations written for Ben and Claire.

Ben took the mic (yes, there was a mic all along) from Sid and started beatboxing before initiating round two.

Before I was a boring old Midwestern dad,
I used to be a rad Chad who'd vacationed in
    Baghdad,
on a college trip! Picture this:

Hallucinating on shrooms, playing Doom on
    my Sega Genesis!
My generation came up with the stuff your
    generation takes for granted,
acting like Ella from Ella Enchanted when
    you get five likes!
Yikes! We used to go on hikes, do wheelies on
    bikes,
while you lot stay inside and thumb your
    Xbox controller!
Call me steamroller, unh! Cuz I destroyed
    these kids!

The crowd cheered and clapped. They suddenly started making way for a big white bench. On the other side of that bench sat Eminem, Snoop Dogg, and Lil Wayne with notepads in front of them. They were judging this battle. A helicopter soared above, and a reporter with an abysmally large camera live-streamed the whole thing to CNN. The FOX News truck was trying to make its way past the frenzied fans now pitching tents in the cul-de-sac.

It was Tara's turn.

Your infantile clap-back isn't gonna get you
    clout, kids,

remember, when you're being obnoxiously
    loud, kids,
You're being a little extra, I'm gonna call you
    out, kids!
Words like finna ain't gonna get you chicken
    dinna!
and saying something is G.O.A.T is just a
    useless flex!
Half of your words can't even pass
    grammatical checks
and balances set in place by the authorities,
so please keep your lingo to your frats and
    sororities!

"All right! That's enough!" Eminem yelled.

"That's right, now we judge," Snoop Dogg said as he inhaled a deep one from his fat blunt. "Mm. Sweet dope, fo shizzle."

"Word," Lil Wayne said.

The three of them started comparing notes, whispering to each other, and then Eminem stood up, mic in hand:

Now, this rap battle, it was a fierce one, I'll admit.
Both sides had plenty to say. But after consulting

with my fellow judges, and looking at the polls online, it's so clear that the whole thing remains divided. Half the people have voted for Sid and Tara, while the other half is clearly in support of Ben and Claire. Me, personally, I think this generational rap battle is stupid, but who cares about what I think? I'm just Eminem, one of the greatest rappers of all time.

Overhead, an airplane with a huge banner saying "We love you for your down-to-earth attitude, Mr. Eminem" flew across the sky.

Snoop Dogg took the mic from Eminem and said:

Today was a groundbreaking day in history. A regular, small town like Urbana became the ground zero for a generational war of words between these two Gen-X'ers and these two Gen-Z kids. But I must say, we all learned a valuable lesson today. Neither generation is better than the other. It all comes to down to individual choices and the paths we take toward being better humans.

Everyone present did a loud "aww."

"Now it's time for giveaways!" Lil Wayne screamed and everyone lost their moment of sobriety and began cheering wildly:

> Ben, your powerful lines moved us, and so we're giving you and your wife a six-month paid vacation to the Bermudas!" Lil Wayne said, to much applause. "Claire, we saw on your online wish-list that you wanted seven-hundred thousand dollars to pay off your student loans and buy a nice little beachfront house in Florida. You also mentioned that you wanted scholarships for your kids. We're feeling awfully generous today, so we're going to give you one million dollars in cash!

Claire fainted. Luckily, there was an ambulance parked just outside their house. Two medical professionals came with a stretcher and took her away. Ben followed not too far behind, tears of joy all over his face.

"Now kids," Eminem took the mic from Lil Wayne:

> We heard your lyrics loud and clear and we want to reward you just as much as we've rewarded your parents. Sid, your Instagram account is

basically one huge fan account of the Sony PlayStation 5 and all of its games. So, not only did we get you the latest PlayStation 5, but after getting in touch with MIT, we've given you a full-ride scholarship to study game development and design at, you guessed it, MIT!

Sid was weeping with joy, on his knees, holding on to his head, questioning the reality he was living.

"Tara, you're the biggest Demi Lovato fan, from what we've assumed after reading your Tumblr. Guess who's here as well?"

A purple cloud of awesomeness blew up (a magnificent unicorn flew in the air) and Demi Lovato, in all her glory and splendor, appeared out of thin air, as splendid as ever. Tara had a fan-girl moment and began screaming loudly, running in circles. She leaped onto Demi and hugged her tight. Demi took the mic from Eminem:

Tara, you're a very powerful lyricist. So, it only makes sense that you record an entire album with me and keep half the money from the sales! Trust me, I'm Demi Lovato. We're going to get a lot of sales. What I, Demi-Actual-Lovato, am trying to say is, you're going to be very rich and famous.

* * *

Five months later, the entire family is sitting in their summer outfits on a beach in Bermuda. They're sunbathing out in the white sand, in front of the pristine blue beach. Seagulls are cawing in the air. Dolphins are leaping in and out of the water. Sea turtles are unsuccessfully chasing crabs in the shallow part of the water. Sid is sipping from a comically large coconut. Tara is taking pictures for her Instagram account. Mr. and Mrs. Wilson are reading Dan Brown novels, enjoying a nice life.

"And to think this all started because we were worried about the Gen-Z slang our kids were using," Ben says to Claire.

"Yes, honey. One might think that we were living in a fictional world," Claire says, smiling. Her teeth gleam in the sunlight.

"Don't be foolish, dear. We're not fictional characters. We're just good, understanding parents, and we have these perfect, law-abiding, responsible children," Ben says.

But the nightmares will haunt him from that day on, making him question the realness of his fragile reality. Is he a character? He will never know.

CPSIA information can be obtained
at www.ICGtesting.com
Printed in the USA
BVHW031556131021
618739BV00021B/170